Horse

Beginners

Ownership, Training, Leadership and Safety Basics

Dave Wyatt

This book is dedicated to anyone interested in owning, training, riding and enjoying the companionship of a horse. Every horse expert started out as a beginner so be smart and not intimidated when it comes time to saddle up.

TABLE OF CONTENTS

PUBLISHER'S NOTES

Disclaimer

This publication is intended to provide helpful and informative material. It is not intended to diagnose, treat, cure, or prevent any health problem or condition, nor is intended to replace the advice of a physician. No action should be taken solely on the contents of this book. Always consult your physician or qualified health-care professional on any matters regarding your health and before adopting any suggestions in this book or drawing inferences from it.

The author and publisher specifically disclaim all responsibility for any liability, loss or risk, personal or otherwise, which is incurred as a consequence, directly or indirectly, from the use or application of any contents of this book.

Any and all product names referenced within this book are the trademarks of their respective owners. None of these owners have sponsored, authorized, endorsed, or approved this book.

Always read all information provided by the manufacturers' product labels before using their products. The author and publisher are not responsible for claims made by manufacturers.

Print Edition 2014

CHAPTER 1: HORSES 101

You are reading this book because you are thinking about purchasing a horse or you already have one. With each scenario, you will need to think about horse training. It does not matter if you do it by yourself or get a professional to do it for you.

Since you have already made a horse purchase you know that it costs anywhere from one to twenty thousand dollars. You might have various things fixed into your budget such as shoeing, feeding and medical care. You have probably figured this to be about two thousand each year, which will only apply if you are a property owner in the country and the horse is on your property. If you want to board your horse, then you should put an extra two to three thousand more into your budget.

If you want to ride your horse for about 350 hours annually, the cost will be the expenses that you have already accounted for in addition to things such as sick days and health insurance. You might be wondering about the sick days and insurance and this is the explanation. A lot of people get hurt when they ride their horses. Around twenty-five percent of these people are children under the age of 16. Unfortunately, many of these accidents result in brain damage to the rider.

Obviously, brain damage can have a lifetime effect. These are not the types of injuries that happen during professional riding at rodeos. These are the kinds of injuries that occur because people ride horses for pleasure. Around eighty percent of these accidents happen at regular riding speeds and are not caused because the horse was afraid and bucked a person off.

Sadly enough, you are much safer on the back of a motorcycle than you are riding horseback. Reports say that motorcycle riders who have accidents have had an average of 7000 hours of riding time. The same reports show that for horseback riders who have accidents, they have ridden an average of 350 hours.

The best way to stop accidents is to get as much knowledge as you can. If you train your horse, he probably will not have bad behavior. He will not be an unruly animal that causes plenty of accidents and injuries. You can avoid behaviors such as a horse that likes to kick, run wild or bite the rider. An experienced horse will know how to work with an experienced rider.

Riding horseback on a horse that has not been trained is very dangerous. It can be compared to driving a car that has lost control of the brakes. You can go for a joy ride, but it might not have a happy ending. The horse does not plan on harming you, but if he does not know what to do, you are putting yourself into a lot of danger. A horse is a huge animal that can do whatever he pleases. When it comes to investing your money, owning a horse is a large liability. The horse can cause harm to others and if or when you decide to sell, you rarely get your money back.

If your horse is not trained, he could be considered dangerous. You purchased a horse for a reason. Keep in mind that proper training makes it easier for you to use your horse. Also he will be a safer horse when trained. If you do not have the knowledge or time to train a horse, then get a horse trainer. Each horse is different so it can take anywhere from two to twelve months to properly train a horse. You will end up with a horse that has received the correct training but you won't be trained.

It is cheaper to train your own horse. During training you cannot actually ride your horse. However, you will gain knowledge and hands on experience.

The following are some tips if you are a new horseback rider

- If you have never owned a horse before, hire a professional trainer that can help you pick out a good horse.

- Never leave children unsupervised when horses are around. Be certain that children not in the path of a horse if he chooses to kick.

- Teach children about horse safety. Purchase a saddle that has numerous catches so that if you fall out of the saddle, the horse will not drag you around if your feet get stuck in the stirrups.

- Get an equestrian helmet that meets the requirements of ASTM.

- Do not let your horse kiss you because this can turn into biting, which is difficult to stop.

- Make sure that your clothes are form fitting and do not get caught on fences or branches.

- Do not try to surprise a horse from the behind.

Chapter 2: Tips On Buying A Horse

There is a very important step you shouldn't skip before you make the decision to purchase a horse. Have a trusted vet accompany you and take a look at the animal before you sign off on the deal. The vet can give you details about the horse during the examination and answer any questions you might have about the animal. If the vet feels that the horse would not be a good fit for you, it's important that you respect their decision.

The vet may notice that the horse has a difficult temperament or is perhaps lacking in the training basics that would make him a good purchase for a first time horse owner. He may also recommend that a cutting horse that is very well trained may not necessarily be the best option for you if your goal is to have a riding horse. This is because that animal has been trained to do another job entirely.

The fee that you pay the vet is for much more than just the check-up, as it is also for his expertise and knowledge. There will be those that will tell you that a vet doesn't have the right qualifications to match you with a horse, but they will know the animal and its potential behavior better than anyone. If you do take a vet with you, listen to his opinion and respect his professional advice. There might even be a situation where he believes the horse will be a good purchase, but that a professional trainer may be required afterwards.

It is normal for the seller to be present during the examination. The vet will generally ask that they remain quiet as it's natural that the seller would try to influence your final decision.

One of the first things the vet will check for are physical issues. If a horse has a medical problem or a pre-existing condition, it may not make him a suitable animal for your specific needs. For example, if you are predominantly after a riding horse, you wouldn't want one that has leg problems that make him impossible to ride. You also don't want to end up with a horse that will end up incurring large vet bills down the road.

If you are aware of an existing health problem that the horse has, ask the vet to check on this condition. He may decline to do so, but will let you know of the potential problems the condition may bring. One issue you may encounter is when you ask the vet to examine a horse that belongs to an existing client. Many will see this as a conflict of interest, and decline.

There are plenty of people who would sooner not listen to what anyone has to say, and who will simply purchase a horse on their own without the vet check-up. If you fall into that group and are about to purchase a horse, you should know that choosing the wrong animal could potentially end up costing you tens of thousands of dollars when issues start to arise that you never knew about.

CHAPTER 3: THINGS THAT HORSE OWNERS DO INCORRECTLY

Thinking That All Horses Are Easy To Ride

No two horses are exactly alike. Some will let you ride them without any problems. However, others are so new that you could get hurt if you are also a newbie. Mature horses will usually let anyone ride them because they have had a lot of riders over the years and know what types of mistakes can be made. The younger ones are more of a challenge unless someone has already broken them in.

Thinking That There Is One Specific Way to Train a Horse

When a horse owner with experience has horse problems he will ask others for help. They will normally start with books. When the author talks about one particular strategy, the horse owner makes the assumption that this one strategy is used by all horse trainers. When he tries to use the strategy and it does not work, then he thinks that his horse cannot be trained. Obviously, there are numerous horse training methods. If one does nothing for you then use something else. Just find another book with another training method.

Not Riding the Horse Enough

If you are a new horse owner and are having problems with your horse, there might not be anything wrong with the horse. The problem might be that you have not taken the time to ride him more often. You must ride a horse in order for it to be a good riding horse. So start riding him more often. Riding him a few weeks out of the year is not enough time to ride.

Assuming That the Horse Is the Problem

Horses have flaws just like any other animal. However, many of the problems that you have with your horse are your fault, not the fault of the horse. Analyse your problem and determine who is at fault. You might find that you don't have enough control over your horse.

You Don't Know How Your Own Horse Thinks

Horses are different from cats and dogs. So, don't assume that they are going to act or think like cats and dogs. Horses are known to run away from things that make them scared. This has been a part of their nature for years. Horse training requires an owner who is patient and understands that horses are naturally frightened by most things.

You Fail To See That Your Horse Can Be Taught Something during Each Interaction

It does not matter if you rub, brush or groom him. Each time that you come into contact with your horse, you are training him in some type of way. Since you are a new horse owner, you should be aware of the things that you do around your horse. Unlike a child, your horse will gradually learn things from you. You can impact his behaviour more than what you may think.

If You Don't Have the Time to Learn To Ride and You Are Inexperienced, Your Riding At This Point Can Cause a Lot of Unwanted Problems

A lot of new horse owners want to ride their horse even though they do not have horse riding experience. Horses respond to things such as leg pressure, how a rider sits in the saddle and the mood of the rider. So you should understand what the riding process entails.

If you want to provide successful horse training, it is imperative that you learn everything that you can about your horse. If you are an inexperienced rider, take lessons before mounting your horse. Also, understand his thinking and how to deal with horse behavior. Most importantly, you must ride a horse consistently in order for it to become a good riding horse.

CHAPTER 4: ADVICE FOR NEWBIE TRAINERS

Horse training is a slow process where you must get your horse's attention and teach him via commands. You want your horse to see you as the lead mane. It does not matter what your or the horse's gender may be. However, if your horse has a natural instinct to lead, you might find horse training to be a challenge.

Obviously, your horse will want an owner that can train him and tell him what needs to be done. After all, a horse is a herd animal. Thus, you must take the rein and lead. The horse will follow you because he either respects or fears you. However, try to get your horse to respect you as a result of what is done whenever the two of you communicate with one another.

Usually, a horse will not start training until he is around two years of age. However a foal can learn at any age. If you spend a lot of time with your horse, he will not only get more familiar with you, but also with people in general.

When your horse is old enough for training, you should start with the simple stuff. This is not the time to ride him. The horse is not ready for this as of yet. It is time to lunge him, or ground train him with a lead rope. This should be the first step of your training journey. The line of a lunge connects to a horse halter and lets the horse move around in circles while he is given various commands.

You should also show your horse how to walk alongside you with a lead. Lead training involves commanding the horse to stop and turn. This is very important and is usually needed every day. A lot of horses will try to test you and see what they can get away with doing lead training. The number one thing that they like to do is shoulder you out of their space. This should never be tolerated. If he refuses to go through this basic training, it will almost be impossible to continue training.

A horse has to be trained so that he gets used to the fact that he will have a rider. Basically, he has to be broken. He has to learn how to interpret your signals and follow them. Thus, he must react to your commands. This should be done so that you don't have to use whips or crops to punish him for disobeying you. Training sessions do not have a specific time limit, which means they can be as long or short as you want them to be. But, account for the needs of the horse. He needs to have a balance.

Use the first couple of minutes of the training session as warm up time. This is needed for both physical and mental reasons. The horse has to warm up his joints and muscles and lunging is usually used for this purpose.

The second training session should also include training that the horse got in the first session. Adding new skills will be a small change to the training that your horse received previously. Layering these skills is the most effective way to train your horse.

When you get a new saddle, you want your horse to know about it. But, remove it from his sight after a couple of minutes. Do this for a few days at a time. You want the horse to become familiar with the new item and not be frightened by it. Then allow your horse to wear the saddle while he is doing a warm up lunge. When he gets used to the new saddle, get someone to sit on him. Then let him lunge with someone on his back. Add new items, but just for a short time period.

Also think about doing the same thing when adding the bit. Do it gradually. A horse has to be accustomed to a bit being in his mouth. The saddle process was long and drawn out and this will be too. The horse has to get used to a strange object being in his mouth while he is trying to swallow his saliva. To make this process a little easier, you have to put the bit into the horse's mouth for a couple of minutes and gradually go through the process until he gets used to the strange item in his mouth.

As stated earlier, the saddle has to be put on him gradually. You have to take off the stirrups and leathers as the first step. Allow the horse to see the saddle and hold it over him. If he is still afraid of the saddle then do not let it touch him. You will probably have to rub and stoke him a lot when you first put the saddle on him. Each time you put the saddle on him, add a new piece of equipment such as the girth, leathers and stirrups. Once again, you cannot add a new piece of equipment until the horse is no longer afraid of the last item that was added. You have to have a lot of patience for this process because it will be very time consuming.

Remember to end your training session with a cool down. Always begin with a warm up and end with a cool down. Start the cool down when everything is going well and way before your horse gets irritated with the training. This will help your horse in both a physical and emotional manner. The cool down period helps the horse to see the training sessions as good. So, his last memory of the experience should be a good one. At this point, let him play a bit and then send him back to the stable.

Remember that your horse's behavior is influenced by you, so you must remain patient and fearless at all times. This will help to calm your horse down as well. Whatever you do, the horse will be able to sense what you are doing. You are the lead mare that will teach him. Whenever he figures out your various cues and commands he will have no problem following you.

When it comes to horse training there are specific guidelines that you can follow. It has been called both an art and a science.

Horse training should not be repetitive if the horse does what you want. Do not repeat a command too many times if it is done right. Doing so will cause the horse to not want to do them anymore. Do not practice the commands until you run them in the ground. Stop and start another day with the same commands. Once he learns one command, work on others. The training session should not get boring or irritating to the horse. If this happens, then future training sessions will be almost impossible.

Also, you want to determine what your horse's mood is when you start the training. You want to know what is going on with his mood before you train him.

Give the horse praise if you think that he feels uneasy. You want him to be high spirited so that you can continue to rub and praise him. However, be cautious if you plan to utilize aids during this time.

If your horse is stubborn, then you must have patience and a strong sense of commitment to work with him. Still work at those commands and get him to do what you want.

If you know what his temper is like before you start the training, your training will be much more successful. It is crucial that you do not miss this step in the very beginning.

If you want the process to go much smoother, you must do whatever it takes to help your horse learn. You can accomplish this by having a better understanding of your horse and what his needs are overall.

CHAPTER 5: THE KEY TO HORSE TRAINING

Horses don't know how to reason. This is why it is hard to train them. In order to train successfully you have to understand their thought process. This is the only way to determine if your training methods are actually working.

Successful horse training is based upon fear and punishment. This is how horses have been trained for centuries. Horse trainers have learned to use the combination of fear and punishment as a way to get horses to do what they want them to do.

You know that the horse is scared, but you cannot abuse it as a result of this knowledge. Going too far can have a negative impact that will never work in your favor. If anything goes wrong, you are going to have problems training the horse.

The horse must have confidence in you. This is one of the first things that you have to teach your horse. If the horse has no confidence in you, he will never learn how to trust you. Confidence and trust are the most important things about horse training.

There are numerous ways to make your horse gain confidence in you. The following method is one of the simplest ways to make this happen, and it has been in existence since the 1800s.

This lesson about confidence leverages the horse's fear, but it never takes it for granted. Fear is controlled and utilized in a manner that will make the horse gain confidence in you. It is somewhat like making a child watch a horror movie while you hold and protect him.

If the horse is frightened, you need to be around to provide protection and let him know that all is fine. This can be done by rubbing him and talking to him in a soothing tone. In the end, the horse will see you as a superhero and he will continuously rely on your strength.

The following example shows this. Just imagine that you are horse riding with a group of people and the group rides upon a creek. All of the other horses readily cross the creek. However, your horse refuses to cross the creek.

You get mad and start booting your horse's ribs. The horse wants to cross the creek just like you want him to, but he is afraid of the running water. Out of fear, the horse begins to prance back and forth. He sniffs the water, but he will not cross the creek. All during this time, you are constantly booting him in the ribs.

If you had stepped back from the situation for a while, you would have realized that the horse was not doing this on purpose. The horse was just afraid. The horse needed your superhero powers at this time. He needed your help. You should have rubbed him and talked to him in a calm and relaxing voice.

Because you were so frustrated and did not step back and analyze the situation, you just made things even worse. You made the horse even more afraid of the creek's rushing water. Now instead of just being afraid of rushing water, the horse thinks that he will receive a punishment also.

Now, think about how the horse sees this scenario. View it from his eyes.

As a horse, you don't know how to reason. You just know how to survive. Fear is one of the main things that keeps you alive each and every day. If you are scared of something, you instinctively know how to run from it. Being afraid is a survival tactic.

Now let's go back over what happened based upon what the horse was thinking. You are at the edge of the creek and the water is rushing by. You aren't going to cross the water because you think that it is dangerous. In addition, the person who is riding you is mad because you refuse to cross the water. As a result, he won't stop kicking you in the ribs.

As a horse, you are afraid of the rushing water and you hate the punishment that you are receiving. You want to do as your rider wants, but instinctively you cannot proceed because you think that danger is present.

As the rider, you should have known that your horse was scared and that he was not disobeying you on purpose. This was just his instinctively behavior.

You should have talked to him in a calming voice and rubbed him. You should have even guided him to the water and let him sniff it first.

Since you did not take the right steps, your horse is now scared and confused. In addition, he feels like you punished him. As a result, your horse no longer trusts you. There could have been a happier ending to this story if you had been proactive. Keep in mind that your horse is depending on you to always be there to protect and console him. This means that you have to know the difference between when he is trying to disobey you and when he is actually scared out of his mind.

CHAPTER 6: HORSE TRAINING AND VOICE COMMANDS

If you are an experienced horse trainer, then horse commands are probably just simple words to you. However, to the horse, they are a series of sounds. Horses cannot reason and do not know the human language. So, think of some sound you can use whenever you want your horse to react.

For instance, take the word "whoa." This word is extremely overused. This command tells the horse to stop. However, some riders like to use this command just for the purpose of slowing down the horse. The horse learns to slow down when he hears this command as opposed to coming to a stop. The horse owner then blames the horse and thinks that he does not understand commands, but he is the one who has caused the problem.

If you give the horse a command that stands for something other than what you want him to do, then you are telling your horse a lie. This is not the right strategy to use. So, never do this because it will be a waste of time. This means using the command "whoa" when you want him to stop and not when you want him to slow down.

Your voice commands should only have a few syllables. So, if you want your horse to back up then the command "back" will do just fine. If you want him to walk then say "walk" and so on.

Create voice commands so that they correspond to a particular action. If you want to train your horse on how to gallop, then pick out an aid that will teach him how to gallop. Use it whenever you are in the round pen. When you opt to use the word "gallop," use an aid so that it will push the horse to go faster.

If you want to teach your horse how to walk, then go in the opposite direction in the round pen and walk. If the horse goes too fast, then give the walk command and this will make him decrease his speed. You could also move a little bit in front of him, which will also indicate to him to decrease speed. Once he has gone round the pen a couple of times, then you should rub him and talk to him.

However, be aware of how you talk to your horse. Do not make the commands sound as if you are yelling at him. This will just frighten or confuse your horse. Also, it will be difficult to continue training, which will cause a break in training. Training will just linger on longer and this will just frustrate you even more.

One of the more popular horse training commands is "step." This command is utilized when you want your horse to take a step forward. Do not use this command in a threatening or forceful voice. Your horse will think that you are trying to punish him. As a result, your horse will need more time to figure out what you want him to do.

CHAPTER 7: HOW TO GET YOUR HORSE TO OBEY AND RESPECT YOU

Just like in the armed forces, there is a definite pecking order in nature. When you enlist, the ranks go from General down to Private. The General is the one who will give the orders about what needs to be done and who needs to do it.

The person directly below the General will act like the top dog to his subordinates, but he still has to answer to the General above him. A similar pattern goes on all the way down the ranks. This is similar to how things work in the animal kingdom, which is something that you can actually put to good use. You need to be the General to your horse so that he will look to your for instruction and be obedient.

Natural instinct will see a dominant horse look to someone more dominant for leadership. That dominant one needs to be you. One of the best ways to do this is through body language that exudes confidence. Make sure not to cross the line to dominance and aggression, as neither will work.

A horse that acts like a General will need you to be very assertive, but you also need to ensure that he does not view you as a threat. There is a fine line between assertion and threatening behavior, and the horse will put up a fight if he senses that you are threatening. That is a fight you will lose every time.

Wild horses that are naturally dominant and aggressive will tighten their bodies and rapidly move with anger to invade the space of another horse. The weaker horse will quickly give up that space to the more dominant horse. This behavior is akin to the General barking and order and the Private jumping to obey.

When the horses are relaxed, they will perform the same actions, albeit in slow steps. This slow movement will attract other horses to a space, which is how they welcome one another into their space.

When your horse looks at you with pinned ears and a clamped-down tail, it is his way of showing that he thinks he is the General. In order for you to assume the General role, you are going to have to get him out of his space. You need to strike first and match all his moves with matching moves of your own.

One way to do this is to make quick, fly-swatting arm movements in his direction. If he continues to adopt an aggressive stance and behavior, you should also adopt an aggressive tone of voice when addressing him.

You will know you've won when his head turns or drops, or when he relaxes his tail and takes deep breaths. This is a sure sign that he is ready and willing to stop and listen to what you have to say. It is incredibly important that you pay attention to all the signs, as it is only then that you will see that the horse has given you the reins as General and is ready to accept his role as the Private.

Winning that first battle is not the end, though, and you need to see how he reacts when you start to train him. Swinging his rear end at you or rubbing his head on you is a sign that he is challenging you. Make sure that you are never threatening, as you do not want to end up with a horse that lacks confidence.

CHAPTER 8: LEAD ROPE TRAINING FOR HORSES

The lead rope that you see attached to the horse's halter does nothing to control the horse. This means that it cannot be used to control or lead the horse. It is just used to tell the horse the shape, direction and speed that he needs to move in.

The stop command is one of the simplest ones to teach a horse. You can do this by walking the horse, coming to a complete stop and giving him the stop command. When you stop, do not pull or tug on the lead rope. All is needed is a little stiff pressure.

The horse's front will probably stop and the back will move a fourth of a circle. As time goes on, he will learn to stop both of his front and back legs.

The first few lessons should go no longer than ten or fifteen minutes. This type of training is something that you can teach your horse even when he is a foal.

Begin by teaching him in a smaller indoor setting. By using an indoor setting, there won't be as many interruptions as there would be in an outdoor setting. Thus, you will find it much simpler to make the horse concentrate on what you are doing and saying.

The first few times in this new setting will make your horse curious about his surroundings. Give him some freedom to run around and play in his new setting. Don't try to control him at this point. Just let him play and stick close behind him.

If you are creative enough you could turn this play time into an actual lesson. With just two continual movements you can start two things that your horse will eventually understand. When you are walking in the same direction as the horse, you are teaching him the direction that is needed for him to move forward. When you are facing the horse, you are showing him how to stop and stand.

Once he knows what these two things are, you can change from being in front of his shoulder to being in front of him going in the same direction. You will have the chance to coax him into walking with you. This is done by moving your feet in an obvious manner. As time goes on you can build upon these skills and learn how to lead the horse forward or get him to stop on command.

It is essential that you show your horse how to back up. Do not assume that it is just about backing up by one step. Hold the reins and place your weight backwards. Whenever he walks backwards, loosen the grip. Do this in order to get him to back up for whatever amount of time is needed.

If you teach and give your horse certain commands that always mean the same thing each time, your horse will figure out what needs to be done. It does not matter if it is trying to lead him into the trailer or if you are trying to lunge him.

CHAPTER 9: LEADING YOUR HORSE TO GET CONTROL

Controlling a horse by pulling them around with a lead rope is a technique attempted by many. It ends up being a tug of war, as the person doing the jerking on the lead rope is met with resistance by the horse that pulls back.

You can use the lead rope to move him around, but you need to make sure that there is plenty of slack so that he doesn't feel as though he is being jerked or pulled. If he makes a wrong move, you will need to stop and position his body the right way.

This is why control over his body is so important. The easiest way to achieve that is to move his rear end away from you so that you have control of his feet. This is commonly referred to as disengaging the hindquarters. The reason this works is because you are essentially removing all of the stiffness and tension and making him focus on you.

In order to get him to move his rear end away from you, there are a few things you can try. The most common method is to face his shoulders and point at his hip. If this has no effect, cluck at him while continuing to point. Give him a little tap with the lead rope and cluck some more if he still doesn't move.

Instantly relieve the pressure the moment he does move, be sure to pat him and tell him how good he is. You can then ask for the next move. Continue repeating the process, asking for more and more steps. It is important that you do this on both sides of the body. With regular training, the simple act of pointing at his hip should be enough to get him moving. It will likely take a few days of repetitive training to let him know that you are the boss and in control.

Once he has been moved, you can turn around and start moving forward. You will notice at this point that all of his attention is on you. He will be following your movements and be completely aware of what you are up to. If he gets spooked or distracted, you might need to position his rear end one more time. He will quickly pick up your natural pace and fall in line to keep up with you.

If you find that he moves faster and starts to get ahead of you, move his hindquarters. The same rules apply if he falls off the pace and starts to trail behind. Any movement that goes off your intended path will result in you moving his hindquarters.

Have control of your horse as you lead him is one of the most basic training techniques out there. Teaching him this will lead to the next steps such as getting him into a trailer, bathing, and riding. He will become gentle and responsive to your commands at all times, which will even translate to when you are up in the saddle.

CHAPTER 10: GETTING YOUR HORSE INTO THE TRAILER

Getting your horse inside of a trailer can be very difficult. This is really the case if the horse is not very cooperative. If you do not have the patience to perform this task, or if you find it very frustrating, it can become quite dangerous. Some people in this state of mind will try to push the horse into the trailer when he does not want to get into the trailer. If the horse is scared or irritated, he will lash at you or mash you inside of the trailer. Unfortunately, this might lead to your getting hurt and the horse still being outside of the trailer.

There are strategies that you can use to teach your horse when it comes to trailer loading. Similar to many of the things that you are teaching your horse, the success of this training will rely on your level of patience and how the horse has been treated in the past.

If the horse has had a hard time getting into the trailer in the past, it will take a while to get him used to moving up the ramp and entering a trailer that is spooky, new and dark. However, if you start trying to train him when he is a foal, he will think that loading a trailer is nothing new. He will automatically become accustomed to it.

Because the horse has to walk up the ramp, you should come to a stop at the end and do not move backwards. Basically, you have to train him in baby steps. The first thing that you should do is teach him how to walk. Use a lead rope that has a thirty two inch chain that covers his nose and runs up along his cheeks. In your right hand you should have a dressage whip. In your left hand there should be the lead rope.

Beckon for him to walk by lightly tapping him on the hindquarters. Once he has moved forward by a couple of steps, give him the stop command by saying "whoa." Softly tug on the lead rope to get him to stop. Make him start walking again and when he starts walking, verbally reward him. If he seems unhappy by pushing away or making a sharp turn in front of you, then begin this process once more. Do it again until he has learned how to walk via the command and knows how to stop and does not have to backup to do it. Hopefully, he will walk when you give the command and you won't have to ever use the dressage whip.

It is now time to move on to the trailer training. Now that your horse knows the commands for walk, you have to get him to walk into the trailer. Don't try to lead him into the trailer from the inside. Using that strategy has gotten plenty of people hurt. Your job is to get him to voluntarily walk into the trailer. You might have to walk up the ramp with him part of the way and let him do the rest on his own. He might go part of the way and then attempt to back up. If this is the case, then start the journey once more until he gets it right.

You must have the right mind set to do this. You will also need to be patient with your horse in order to get him loaded into the trailer. If you allow him to get his way, then this will continue and you will never get him into the trailer. So, when he tries to back out down the ramp, remember to be patient with him. Walk back up the ramp with him to the trailer. Let him see that you can do the same thing all day long. Make him see that you will continue walking him up that ramp for as long as it takes to get him into the trailer.

If it is necessary, thump him on the bottom to get him to move. Do not try to use force to get him inside of the trailer because this could lead to harm for you. Also, if he is following the commands, do not hit him. When he does what you want, do not forget to give him some type of verbal reward and allow him to take a break. This will indicate to him that he is doing what you want. This also tells him that you will stop doing the same thing over and over again.

Teaching your horse to walk will not happen overnight. This is a gradual process. Going through the various steps will also be time consuming. Try doing the training at varied times of the day. You will discover that it is just as easy to load at night as it is during the day.

CHAPTER 11: 5 ERRORS THAT HORSE OWNERS MAKE WHEN LOADING HORSES

Treating Your Horse like a Cat or Dog

If a horse owner has not received proper training, he might assume that he can treat his horse like a cat or a dog. Unknowingly he will try to tap on his leg a couple of times and beckon the horse to "C'mon." Unfortunately, he won't get his desired response. The horse is not going to jump into the trailer like an overjoyed little puppy.

Baiting Your Horse with Food

Horse owners will also try to put food such as apples or grain in the front section of the trailer as a way to get the horse inside. Unfortunately, this is a strategy that always fizzles out. If you manage to get your horse into the trailer with this trick, then you are a very lucky person. Now, a few horses might sniff around the food, but they will never step completely into the trailer. So, this food baiting trick is a waste of your time.

Failing to Hook the Truck and Trailer Together

This is usually a mistake that new horse owners make; however, some won't remember to hook the truck and trailer together before they attempt to get the horse inside. Even if the horse did miraculously step into the trailer, the trailer would be unstable. Why? It's because the trailer is not connected to the truck. Now, the horse is frightened. The next time it will be even harder to get him into the truck.

Trying to Pull the Horse into the Trailer

A few horse owners will attempt to tug and pull on the horse in order to get him into the trailer. This never works and usually ends up being a battle between the owner and the horse. Do you really think you're going to win against an animal that is stronger and heavier?

Going Trail Riding Before Learning How to Consistently Load a Horse

A lot of horse owners think that if they can get their horse into the trailer just one time, then they can do it again and again. They assume that they no longer need training. However, the smart thing to do is to continue training and use signals that will tell your horse what needs to be done. The efficiency of the training will depend on the communication between the owner and horse.

If you are still finding it difficult to get your horse into the trailer, then try doing the following. Loop a long rope over his rear and allow it to fall down until it gets to the top of his hind legs. Allow the rope to hit his hind legs and wait to see how he reacts to this. Hold the rope with your right hand while you hold the horse halter with your left hand. Most likely he will try to kick the rope. However, if he does not kick at it, this indicates that he is not worried about where the rope's location.

If he does kick towards the rope, he will just have to take a while and get used to it. Just wait a few minutes and allow the rope to touch his hind legs. Expect him to jump around and try to move away from the rope. He might even try to move around in a circle. While you are holding onto the horse halter, make your left arm stiff. Force him to walk around you while you are holding onto the rope and halter.

Eventually he will come to the conclusion that the rope is not causing any pain. At this point, he won't have any problems with your going on to the next step. Make him move in your direction by pulling on the rope. While he is moving forward and away from your pull, loosen up your grip. Make him see that he should move when you increase the pressure. It should not take him long to understand what you want him to do.

Now move him towards the trailer. If need be, guide his head into the trailer. Since the lead rope is on the halter, you can pull on it at the same time that you are pulling on the hind rope. Most likely, the horse will not voluntarily jump into the trailer. But then again, he could. However, be very cautious when you are trying to do this. Your horse could quickly jump into the trailer and accidentally hurt you.

It is hard to get a horse loaded into a trailer and making these mistakes can cause a lot of frustration or even bodily harm. However, if done correctly, your horse will end up in the trailer and you can call it a day.

CHAPTER 12: TRAINING CAN HELP WITH BEHAVIORAL ISSUES

If you have no experience in training horses, the whole process may seem like one big mystery. Things become even more complicated when behavioral problems arise. The average owner can quickly become frustrated, failing to realize that the problem may actually be theirs and not the horses.

The first thing you need to do is figure out what is causing the horse to behave a certain way. For example, your horse may be spooked by the slightest little thing. This is a sign of nerves and feeling as though something is after them, making for a scary ride for both the horse and rider.

Let's imagine for a moment that it's the rider who is causing the horse to become spooked. The key is to then find out what specifically is triggering that issue. New riders will often be tense in the saddle, which a horse will immediately recognize. When the rider is visibly tense, the horse will often react in kind, with that sort of behavior often very habit forming. The fact that the horse is now spooked will cause the rider to become even more tense, all of which exacerbates the problem further.

The rider has the human advantage of being able to reason and get over the fears that are affecting him and the horse. If this is the problem for you, it's important to learn to relax and loosen up in the saddle. The horse will recognize this shift and will alter his behavior and become more confident. The moment that you are both able to relax, the more pleasurable the riding experience will be for you both.

You need to be aware that you are essentially training the horse every time you hop in the saddle.

Every single interaction with your horse counts as training.

The more you encourage him, the better he will react. If you are consistent in your praise, his good behavior will become a habit. If you are consistently tense and rigid, the horse is more likely to be nervous and easily spooked.

That is just one of the problems that could alter the behavior of your horse. This is not always the case, but looking at your own behavior is often a great starting point in diagnosing the behavioral issues of your horse.

CHAPTER 13: HOW TO TEACH YOUR HORSE LONGER SLIDING STOPS

Once you see that your horse has mastered stopping in a single stride and sliding for a couple of feet after being commanded to stop, you can teach him a longer sliding stop. It is essential that your horse has a good grasp of the short sliding stops before taking him to the next level.

There are a few elements that go into establishing the length of the horses slide, such as:

- His natural stopping ability
- The condition of the ground underfoot
- The shoes he wears
- How fast he is travelling when asked to stop
- The rein work, posture, and cues of the rider

All of the above will have an effect on the slide.

Almost every horse has the natural ability to come to deliver a two-footed slide in good conditions. Not every horse will be able to take that ability and extend that slide into fifteen to twenty feet. If this is something that he is going to be able to do, he will require a good deal of ability and desire.

If you have a horse that really isn't keen on learning the long sliding stop, you are going to end up going through training sessions where you both are uncomfortable and unhappy. At the very worst, you could end up instilling feelings of fear in your horse that are hard to undo. Be sure that your horse is in fact willing to learn before you attempt this type of training.

How can you know if he wants to learn? If you found that getting him to stop while he was trotting or in a slow lope was easy, there is a pretty good chance that the long-slide stop might be trainable. All of this is under the assumption that the stop has been advanced gradually and that he has the physical prowess to pull off a hard stop.

If you found that training your horse to stop while trotting or at a slow lope was tough going, there is probably no reason to try to advance that training. He will likely just resist at every turn, which leads to frustration all around.

The condition of the ground is something else that very much comes into play in the horse slide. The wrong ground will never result in a long slide. You should be on the lookout for ground that had a hard, smooth packed base, as well as a couple of inches of loose dirt lying on top. These are the perfect conditions for the horse to slide on without the risk of his hooves digging in too deep. If the ground is uneven, he may hit a rut that could potentially cause him to be injured.

The couple of inches of loose dirt will lessen the impact of his feet on the hard base, once again reducing the risk of injury. He will be easily able to slide right through that loose stuff. If it's too heavy or is any deeper, he will likely labor to slide through it. He would also need a remarkable amount of strength to do so.

You can make the sliding ground that much better by adding rice hulls or shavings, both of which add a lighter, fluffier feel to the top layer.

The shoes that your horse wears can also play a major role in how far he can slide. Shies that are made of tempered, flat iron bar are the best for sliding. These are generally in the region of an inch to an inch and a half in thickness. The width of the shoe also matters; a wider shoe is better suited to sliding since they provide less friction.

The nails in the shoe should be countersunk as to be flush, which again helps keep friction to a minimum. A quarter inch at the front of the shoe should be curved upwards, much like you would see with a snow ski. This little curve will reduce the risk of the toes of the horse catching in the ground as they slide. The quarters of the shoe should extend back in almost a straight line from the curve at the front, as this will allow for the easy passage of dirt out the back.

The trailers should extend back to the bulbs of the foot, but should not go beyond. The hind feet should be trimmed so that they have longer toes and a lower heel. This method of trimming will deliver a larger surface area on the hooves and make sliding that much easier for the horse. It has the dual effect of reducing the risk of him catching his toes and being hurt. As much as these little changes will help, keep in mind the "less is more" theory. Taking the trimming too far may cause the horse to pull a tendon while sliding to a stop. If you go too low with the heel trimming, it could be his hamstring at risk.

The physical build of your horse is another important factor. A horse with straight hind legs and feet that point straight ahead is a good candidate to be a long slider, as their feet will almost naturally stay together through the duration of the slide. If the horse has back feet that toe out, his hind legs will start to spread the further he slides, which will cause him to pull out of it to get those legs back together where they belong.

Horses that have this problem will leave slide tracks in a V shape. You can correct this problem by turning the horseshoe in a way that will get it to point straight ahead. Rocking the toe a little towards the inside of the foot might also help.

Speed plays a major role, and is perhaps the most important element in the length of the slide. If you are looking to take you horse on a slide that covers the length of an arena, you will start him out slow and slowly up the pace with each passing stride until it comes time to ask him to stop.

The horse should still be accelerating when you deliver the command to stop. This is because he will have his shoulders elevated and his feet further back beneath him, both of which will help him achieve a longer slide.

You need to be paying close attention to his acceleration, as you don't want him to be traveling too fast when you ask him to stop. Chances are he will ignore the command altogether. His natural instinct is to run when you start to open him up, to that point that all of his attention will turn to the run and steer him away from the stop that is about to come. He may also feel that he doesn't have the required strength to stop once he hits a certain speed and he simply won't try. It takes some real practice to find that perfect acceleration point where the stop command yields the best slide results.

Refrain from asking for a hard stop at top speed too often, as he will soon tire of it. Protect his fetlocks at all times by wearing skid boots when you ride.

A poor slide will almost always happen when you have the horse accelerate too quickly and then slow down as the stop approaches. The horse will automatically start to decelerate when you ask for the stop, so this would basically be asking him to do it twice.

The stop command should always be issued on a straightaway and never during a turn. You should also try to ensure that his body is aligned as straight as possible. So imagine seeing a straight line running from the tip of his nose all the way back to the end of the tail before asking him to stop. If you don't he may be off balance, which can end up putting you both down.

The way in which you cue the stop is absolutely crucial. The reins must be in the right position, the timing spot on, and your posture perfect if you want to pull off a long slide. The correct method will deliver great results every time.

A hard pull on the reins will result in a shorter slide, as this will cause the horse to spread his hind legs to far apart, which in turn will lead to him digging deeply into the ground. While the legs do a lot of the work, the neck and head of the horse are crucial to his balance, which is not something that he can achieve if the reins are being yanked on.

There are three different techniques that will help you get this right. The first one should work, but all three may need to be attempted. No two horses react the same way, which is why more than one technique exists. It's up to your to find the one that is the best fit for you and your horse.

As you are approaching the time to issue the stop command, keep the reins slack and say "Whoa!" The horse will feel free to slide for longer, as he will feel that you are not interfering with his movements. Light pressure is all that is required here. With no pulling on the reins, the freedom to slide becomes that much easier. This method will only work if the horse is ready to stop and enjoys the feeling of a long slide. Most horses will happily stop using this technique.

The second method requires you to put a little pressure on the reins as you say "Whoa!" Do not interfere any more once he has started to slide. Again, you are using light pressure and not pulling. Set your hand solid and apply no more than a pound or two of pressure. He will still feel as though the reins are slack and allowing him to slide.

The final technique is one that will work on the vast majority of horses. When you issue the "Whoa!" command, pause for a second before applying pressure on the reins. Your hand should be set to allow a little slack, but no more than an inch or two. The horse will generally react immediately and go into the stop, continuing to slide with the reins slack,

If you feel him start to come out of the stop, set your hand again and slack the reins once more. Continue with the set, slack technique throughout the slide and until the horse comes to a complete stop.

The whoa-set-slack method works because the horse gets the feeling that he is still free from the reins when he first begins to enter the slide. This takes away the feeling of being startled somewhat when the verbal cue and rein pressure are issued at the exact same moment.

Once he has his hooves set and is in the slide, the light pressure of the reins will remind him to stay there. Adding slack to the reins right after that will give him the freedom to keep on sliding. Constant pressure on the reins would have the opposite effect and cause him to bring the slide to a halt too soon.

The horse may try to stop the slide, but the quick set-slack will hold him in there. Don't try to set the reins again unless he shows that he is going to come out of the slide again. The average slide is over quickly, which tells you how rapid the set-slack movement needs to be. You need your full attention to get this right.

The final element in the entire process is the cue to relax your body. You will have used your body to let the horse know you want acceleration, which means you need to stop when you want the horse to do the same. Simply put, you need to sit down, stop all movement, and simply relax your body to the point of being limp in the back, shoulders, and thighs.

Your horse will sense this and recognize it as a cue to stop. That said, there is still the timing to get right. Ride hard until you are ready to cue the stop, as going limp too early will make him stop sooner and result in a shorter slide.

You will also need to practice the posture of your body in order to get the best slide results. Those long, beautiful slides are not something that you are going to achieve in a day or two. Regular practice and adopting the proper techniques will result in long slides eventually becoming the norm.

MEET THE AUTHOR

Horse enthusiast Dave Wyatt helps clients select and train horses. In the suburbs of Chicago, a family in the market for a horse often has little to no knowledge of the process—let's be honest, Chicagoland isn't exactly known for its horse population. Dave knows the value of a great horse, and loves helping families maximize their equine investment.

Dave moved to Chicago in 2011 after living most of his life in scenic Wyoming. After growing up around open spaces and horses, it was quite a culture shock. He missed his childhood horse, and began campaigning and researching to convince his family that Chicago was a great place to house one. Thankfully, they were able to keep their new horse, Sandals at a nearby stable rather than in their tiny garage.

As the only horse owner in his class, he was very popular. At least weekly, he found himself instructing his classmates in how to approach, care for, and ride a horse. No one was surprised when he chose to continue in this on a part time basis and as an author.

These days Dave lives in Barrington, Illinois with his wife and three kids. When they're not out riding, they enjoy camping, great movies and long hikes.

Lightning Source UK Ltd.
Milton Keynes UK
UKHW020144141118
332283UK00008B/151/P